Halden Zimmermann's Guide to High-Impact Blogs for Life Changing Income

By Halden Zimmermann

Contents

Introduction	1
Drawing Up the Blueprints	5
Laying the Foundation	9
Creating a Rough Frame	13
Choosing Unique and Functional Design Elements	17
Navigating the Installation Process	21
Focusing on the Finishing Work	25
Going Over the Punch List	29
Establishing a Presence in the Marketplace	33
Maintenance, Additions and Value Enhancement	37

Introduction

There is so much about the world of blogging that is simply amazing, but perhaps the most fascinating and positive development brought about by its advent is the fact that writers no longer have to conquer a series of increasingly complex obstacles in order to have their work published. Even a literary giant like William Faulkner once found it difficult to find a publisher willing to accept his manuscripts for publication, and he then had to repeatedly battle his publisher over attempts to edit to his work. Editorial oversight was hardly the only issue authors faced, as a great deal of Bruno Schultz's brilliant work was never published during his lifetime, with the bulk of his creative output therefore lost during the great cataclysm of World War II and the Holocaust.

Blogging has made it possible for much of the difficulty associated with being published to be removed entirely, as the blogger is in complete control of every facet of the platform and the content it houses. While this assures that a writer will have a public outlet for creativity, there is no guarantee that the work will reach a broad audience or generate the kind of interest necessary for generating significant income. Promoting the blog's content and creating a profitable writing platform falls entirely on the blogger, but this responsibility also affords a level of control placing the blogger in position to succeed or fail based only on the merit of their individual efforts.

As an executive with a leadership background across a variety of industries, it is my personal opinion that blogging represents one of the great entrepreneurial opportunities of our time. My experience in creating what I like to call "high-impact blogs" has imbued in me a deep understanding of precisely what it takes to be successful as a blogger and to secure a truly life-changing source of income. Through the application of what I have learned during my time as a mechanical engineer, a corporate executive and an author, I believe that the name Halden Zimmermann has come to be synonymous with achievement regardless of the endeavor, as the strategies I have employed throughout my career have served me well in every position I have held. These strategies will therefore serve as the backbone for this book on creating high-impact blogs for generating life-changing income.

High-Impact Blogging

So what exactly is high-impact blogging? Well, the concept is a simple one and is based on the principle that consistent success is only possible when a strong, positive impression is repeatedly made on the audience. In order to build the kind of blog that generates life-changing income, it has to provide information so valuable to the reader that it earns a place among their primary bookmarks. Since most web browsers only have so much space allotted for those bookmarks, the blog you intend to create has to be so impactful that readers are willing to use that limited space as a constant reminder of the value your site possesses. If your blog does not have that kind of immediate and repeated impact on the reader, then it becomes much less likely that it is able to generate the kind of lifestyle-changing income you are seeking.

High-impact blogging does not just refer to the blog's audience. It also refers to you, the blogger. A high-impact blog will change the way you are able to live your life, providing a source of income that does not demand your immediate presence or drain your energy day after day to the point that any time off is spent recovering from work rather than enjoying all that life has to offer. This type of blogging requires a lot of work up front, but the idea is that the blog will continue to pay off long after the work has been completed.

Having worked in leadership positions in a variety of industries, I know just how hard salaried employees work each and every day. I have had the great fortune of being consistently surrounded by highly motivated individuals who care deeply about the quality of their work, and I often imagine the kind of impact these individuals could generate by applying the same level of energy and devotion to blogging. I believe they would experience tremendous success through high-impact blogging and would indeed see their lives positively changed by the kind of income they would surely generate.

Life-Changing Income Defined

It is important to clarify that it is simply not enough to generate more income for it to be considered "life-changing income." In traditional work environments, a promotion includes a pay raise along with increased responsibilities that may place a greater demand on time. Even though we tend to conceive it this way as we seek a promotion, it is indeed rare that someone is paid more while doing less. The same is true for entrepreneurs: generating greater revenue often requires business expansion, and overseeing a larger operation requires more time and energy. So while an increase in pay is indeed a life-changing event, it is not the kind of wholly positive life change we are seeking through high-impact blogging.

I see life-changing income as the kind of income that allows you to radically alter your lifestyle in an overwhelmingly positive manner. This means not just being able to afford a yacht, but also being able to use it at your leisure. I know many CEOs who have yachts of their own that remain anchored for the majority of the year and leave the CEO to long for the time when they will finally be able to experience the beauty and freedom of the open water. The goal of this book is to help you generate the kind of income that allows you to not just afford the finer things in life, but also to have the kind of time necessary to truly enjoy those finer things.

In this guide for creating high-impact blogs for life-changing income, it is my hope that you will learn the practical aspects of blogging from beginning to end. Each chapter covers a different component related to building a high-impact blog, from selecting a high-impact topic to promoting and monetizing the site so that it achieves a life-changing level of revenue. I have attempted to adopt a straightforward approach for the sake of clarity and simplicity, and I truly believe that following each of these steps for building a high-impact blog will allow you to adopt the kind of new lifestyle that lets you enjoy all that life has to offer.

Drawing Up the Blueprints

In discussing the process of building a high-impact blog, I have found that it is helpful to compare the process to that of building a home. From selecting a building site and pouring the foundation to choosing the fixtures and deciding on an interior décor, each step holds a great deal of importance as it relates to the home's value, its ability to function and its inherent potential for growth. There are short-term and long-term factors to consider at each step, and taking shortcuts along the way will surely undermine the quality of the final product.

The same can be said of blogging, as each stage of the process has an impact on all the rest and will play a vital role in the success or failure of the endeavor. A detailed and thoughtful approach is therefore necessary to ensure the best possible outcome, and that begins, of course, with developing a comprehensive plan for bringing your vision to reality. This plan has to be more than just a general outline, and it should instead be much closer to the detail found in a set of blueprints or building plans.

While changes or modifications can be made along the way, having a well thought-out plan taking you from start to finish is an essential component of creating a high-impact blog. When developing this plan, it is important to first consider each of the following questions:

• What is your subject and does it lend itself to high-impact blogging?
• What are your personal blogging goals and how will you measure them?
• How do you intend to turn a profit?
• How much time are you willing to commit?

Answering these questions is a good place to start when

trying to create a comprehensive plan for your blog. Of course, it is helpful to first understand precisely what these questions and answers should entail, so this chapter will focus on addressing these questions for the sake of creating a detailed set of blogging blueprints.

What Gives a Topic "High-Impact" Potential?

I am of the opinion that how you approach your topic is more important than the topic itself, as there is no one subject that is automatically profitable just as there is no subject that makes profitability impossible. If the subject you choose has a very narrow market, then it is important to develop a plan that leverages as much of that market as possible. A detailed plan designed around the specific subject is all that is truly necessary to succeed with a high-impact blog, but those details have to be clearly delineated before any additional steps are taken.

When you choose a topic, consider an intimately familiar subject you feel comfortable discussing at length. While you may see a more expansive market for a DIY blog, creating a site that mimics every other site out there is a mistake that will make it difficult to create any real impact, particularly if you lack the knowledge or experience possessed by other DIY bloggers. If, however, you see that the majority of DIY sites are hosted by experts catering to an audience with a great deal of prior DIY experience, then you may be able to create a high-impact blog by focusing on the part of the audience that has no practical experience with regard to DIY projects. By looking for holes in the market you may find an unfilled niche representing an excellent opportunity for creating a positive impact.

Defining Appropriate and Measurable Goals

One of the most common mistakes made by aspiring bloggers is focusing on lofty goals that can only be achieved over a long period of time. Even when a blogger is making the kind of progress that has them on the path to long-term success and financial security, they will find themselves frustrated that they have not yet achieved their ultimate goal. This is why it is important to set specific short- and long-term goals that are appropriate, achievable and measurable.

Using a series of micro-level plans geared toward achieving different components of a macro-level plan will make it much easier to recognize progress and to feel satisfied that you are well on your way to earning life-changing income. We all want to see immediate results, and having a series of smaller goals leading up to the larger goals makes progress more tangible while simultaneously providing feedback regarding the efficacy of each step of the process.

Outlining a Clear Strategy for Monetization

In order to generate life-changing income, you have to have a clear plan for monetizing your blog right from the outset. I have seen bloggers successfully adopt an approach in which they work on the blog solely as a passion project before they ever consider how to turn a profit, but that does not mean this is the best approach available.

Figuring out how to generate profit after the fact is a dangerous game and you may well end up with an immensely popular site that is unable to leverage its popularity into a profit. When you create a plan for your blog, you have to consider every monetization opportunity so you can ensure that it is properly designed to make the most efficient use of these strategies.

What Kind of Time Commitment Is Necessary?

High-impact blogging focuses on making the most efficient use of your time so that you are able to enjoy a lifestyle of your own creation. That will not be possible if the blog you design requires constant oversight and updates, so your focus should be on creating evergreen content. This means that the information available through your site is relevant and valuable regardless of the day it is posted.

A blog detailing the latest technological advancements, for example, will require constant updates, but a blog that focuses on sustainable organic gardening will contain posts and products that remain valuable for months and years after its original publication. When you choose a topic for your blog, make sure you can tailor the content so that it is evergreen and will only require a minimal time commitment following its initial launch, as this is the best way to ensure the income you generate is not dependent on a continual investment of your time.

Laying the Foundation

The work you put into your blog right from the outset will have a serious impact on how successful it is capable of becoming, and it is for this reason that preparing a strong foundation upon which you can build is an incredibly important part of the early process. How you choose to lay this foundation will primarily depend upon the goals you have set for your blog and how you wish to accomplish those goals, as the manner in which your blog is set up should be a direct reflection of the strategies you intend to use to generate interest in your site along with how you plan to implement your monetization campaign.

Many aspiring bloggers are tempted to focus too heavily on keeping costs down during this part of the process, but this is a mistake that will have a negative impact on the success of the site and will ultimately cost far more to correct had it just been done properly in the first place. This should be looked upon as a long-term investment, and it is particularly important to recognize that the startup costs for a blog pale in comparison to just about any other business endeavor.

When making decisions at this stage of the process, it is certainly acceptable to take costs into consideration. If, however, you find yourself making decisions based mostly on startup costs you are setting yourself up for failure over the long term. Even if you are successful in using a strategy motivated by cutting costs you will ultimately find that your level of success is severely limited by the decisions made in the blog's early stages. Allocate your funds wisely by investing according to your specific blogging goals, as this will eliminate the potential for wasteful spending while giving you the best opportunity for long-term success.

Considerations for Selecting a Web Host

First-timers often jump headfirst into blogging with little planning or preparation, and the first mistake they typically make is in choosing a web host. You have an advantage in this regard, as your unique and detailed blueprints should help you recognize the kind of web hosting you will need in order to meet your personal blogging goals to generate life-changing income. Web hosting is available for free in a number of locations, but these hosts are typically not suited for generating revenue on any significant scale.

Opting for self-hosting should be an automatic decision, as the cost associated with self-hosting is well worth the level of autonomy you are afforded through this type of web host. This may involve shared hosting, dedicated hosting or collocated hosting, and the type you choose will depend on your site design, your traffic goals and your monetization strategies. The cost associated with maintaining the server and being responsible for its continued function is often worth the autonomy it provides, as you will remain in control of security, system resources and the installation of site-specific applications and scripts.

Startup Costs and Developing an Initial Investment Strategy

Certain startup costs are unavoidable out of simple necessity, while others are not nearly as essential from the outset. Web hosting costs are an expenditure that is universally necessary when it comes to high-impact blogging, but there are other startup costs that will vary according to the specific goals and monetization strategies that have been outlined during the initial planning stages. In determining which costs are necessary and which costs are not, it is helpful to ask the following questions:

- How does this specific expenditure benefit the blog?
- Is this cost associated with a feature or function that can be seamlessly integrated at a later date or are there added costs associated with a delay?
- Does this expenditure help achieve a specific blogging goal over a short- or long-term basis?
- What is the potential return on investment for this expenditure?

Each expenditure should have a clear benefit and should play a central role in achieving one of the many goals you have outlined during the planning process. If you question the immediate benefit of an expenditure but see a clear long-term benefit, consider whether the purchase can be delayed without incurring an additional cost as a result of the delay. If you will incur more costs in the long run due to a delay, it is simply best to consider the expenditure a necessity for the long-term benefit of the site. Obviously, the most critical aspect of this is the potential return generated by each expenditure, so make sure you thoughtfully consider how your revenue will be affected by the spending you commit to so early on in this process.

Choosing Among the Many Available Blogging Platforms

The blogging platforms that are now available are incredibly user-friendly, and while you do not have to have any coding experience to run a wildly successful and high-impact blog, it certainly helps if you do have some level of general understanding. This will allow you to customize your site according to your specific wishes and will make it much easier to make structural or functional changes to the site at a moment's notice. It is certainly not a requirement, but taking the time to learn the basics can make a world of difference when it comes to achieving blogging success.

There are a variety of blogging platforms available, with WordPress being perhaps the most popular choice among experienced bloggers. Even though a significant portion of sites use this specific platform, WordPress has enough features and capabilities that each blog appears unique and can be tailored specifically to the unique needs of the blogger.

Of course, WordPress should not necessarily be the default option, as you have to consider the features that are most important to you as it relates to your blogging goals. Consider the capabilities associated with social media promotion, advertising potential and the platform's compatibility with checkout and commenting systems, as each of these aspects will have an effect on the user experience and on the impact you are able to make through blogging.

Creating a Rough Frame

Despite its paramount importance, site layout is a consideration that is often overlooked by bloggers. Even with engaging content and valuable product and service offerings, a blog that is organized in a confusing manner will fail to deliver consistently positive results. After the foundation has been set and the blog is ready to be built in earnest, you must immediately turn your attention to framing your site in a way that is simultaneously unique and familiar. Though those terms are contradictory, it is quite possible to accomplish this vital outcome with relatively little effort.

Familiarity is essential regardless of the industry. It is the reason why tourists are more likely to stop at a franchise restaurant than to try a locally owned establishment, and it is the reason why supermarkets and other businesses apply the same basic store layout in every location. People are simply more comfortable when they are familiar with the look and layout of a place, and that is a fact that businesses recognize and apply with great frequency. This principle can be applied to blogs as well, but it does not mean that your blog should be a carbon copy of a popular blog that covers a subject similar to yours.

The general layout of the site needs to be easily navigated by new readers, and it is therefore important to adopt a layout common to other sites. The overwhelming majority of sites use a basic layout featuring a prominent header directing the reader to different categories within the site. These home pages also tend to have a grid including some combination of images and headlines indicating the most recent or most popular posts, which then lead the reader to a specific post or blog entry. For a high-impact blog, the layout should be familiar enough that readers have no trouble finding their way around, and it should be oriented so that it efficiently converts readers into customers.

Navigating the Site

The goal for your site layout should be to create something that *feels* familiar to a reader without *looking* familiar. The idea is to establish a subconscious feeling of comfort with the way the site is organized without it coming off as being a basic or default blog template. You have to include design elements to make the site unique while maintaining that sense of familiarity, so there is a bit of a balancing act in this regard.

The simplest strategy is to include a branded header linking to the most important pages of your site in a straightforward manner. While it may be tempting to use graphics or icons linking to different pages in the header, it is best to spell everything out so readers are not turned away out of confusion. Even though it may seem entirely obvious which icons lead to a specific page, you cannot assume that readers will universally understand.

A basic site layout should include a variety of pages organized according to a general category. If you have a comprehensive concept that covers a broad range of ideas, make sure you generalize to some degree and opt for sub-categories that fall under the larger category. This will ensure that your header is not crowded with so many categories that readers become overwhelmed by the sheer volume of information. In keeping with this principle, set a limit of five to seven categories to appear in your header, as you can always add a drop-down menu that shows each sub-category.

Attracting Readers and Driving Conversions

When setting up the blog in its initial stages, it is likewise important to consider the strategies you will use for attracting readers to the site for the purpose of generating revenue. With regard to attracting readers, it is always beneficial to employ a variety of search-engine optimization (SEO) strategies. Effective SEO strategies ensure that your blog consistently ranks among the top organic searches, so it is essential to adopt a plan that includes the use of appropriate keywords related to your particular subject.

While organic search ranking is essential, it is certainly not the only way to attract a readership. Guest posts on other blogs generate a greater level of exposure and also raise the profile of your site with regard to both readers and search engines. Writing an unpaid guest post is much more effective than paying for advertising on the same site, as a guest post comes with a tacit endorsement from the blogger hosting your guest post. This is a valuable strategy for enhancing your credibility and bringing in new readers.

Of course, attracting an audience is not enough. With high-impact blogging, you also have to convert these readers into customers. The site layout should gently "push" readers into generating revenue in some way, whether it is by purchasing a product or service you offer or clicking an affiliate link based on your personal recommendation. When laying out the site, consider whether the design will guide readers to a specific outcome so you are able to begin earning the kind of revenue that will provide the opportunity to live the life you have imagined for yourself.

Building a Brand Across Multiple Platforms

A final consideration regarding the layout of the blog has to do with long-term goals. In order to achieve the best possible results, your blog has to be set up so it is able to expand across multiple platforms. When you decide upon a basic layout, you have to make sure that the site is capable of hosting a variety of other platforms like podcasts, videos and social media channels.

It is far more ideal to have a single comprehensive site that includes each of these rather than linking to other platforms away from your blog, so remember to consider long-term goals and potential methods for expansion as you set up your blog for the first time. You may not have immediate plans for podcasting or for setting up a video channel, but it is always best to make it possible to exercise that option should you choose to do so. A brand that extends across multiple platforms is simply more likely to generate truly life-changing income.

Choosing Unique and Functional Design Elements

In the previous chapter we discussed the importance of utilizing a site layout that is easily navigated and is effective with regard to pushing the reader toward a specific desired outcome, which could be anything from the purchase of a product or service to the download of a free digital product in exchange for subscribing to a mailing list. In the chapters that follow, we will discuss the specific monetization strategies available to you, but it is important to first note that the blog's layout and design should be optimized according to your specific conversion goals.

The design elements of the site are certainly a component of the blog's general layout, but it remains essential to discuss how a detail-oriented approach to these elements can have an impact on the success of your blog. These elements contribute to the blog's aesthetics while also affecting its functionality, so it should be quite clear that the implementation of an appropriate design is something to thoughtfully consider.

It is not uncommon for bloggers to take a haphazard approach to design, with many opting to include a variety of elements they find interesting without considering the overarching effect on the whole of the site's design. Just as a home decorated according to several different styles and motifs will appear odd, so too is a blog affected when the totality of the site's design and functionality is not considered as a unified whole. In this regard, form and function must be properly balanced so the site remains easy to use while also achieving a striking and memorable appearance.

Keeping It Clean

When it comes to blog design, a minimalist approach is often best. There have been several studies indicating that decision fatigue often becomes more acute when we are faced with too many options, which then leads to decision avoidance. This concept can be applied to the world of blogging as well, as a reader may be so overwhelmed by the wealth of information a site offers that they avoid making a decision altogether. When you are trying to maximize your conversion rate, the last thing you should want is for readers to be adversely affected by decision avoidance.

It may seem counterintuitive to some, but in this regard less really is more. Keep the site design as clean as possible and keep your posts relatively short to ensure you do not push your readers to a state of fatigue. This will ensure that readers develop an immediate sense of comfort with your site and will be far more likely to contribute to the life-changing income you are seeking to generate though blogging.

Visual Elements

It has long been established that a personal connection is essential when seeking success in any business endeavor. There should be some level of interaction between you and your readers through the blog's comment sections and through social media, but it is highly beneficial to further that connection by including personal elements throughout your site. This does not mean your blog has to become a personal gallery of photographs of you or your friends and family, but there should be something that allows your readers to associate you with a living, breathing human being.

A headshot in the "About" section of your blog will help establish a bit of a more personal connection, but I have always felt that the use of an avatar in the comments section is particularly important. This goes for everyone in the comments section, so make an earnest but polite request for new users to create an avatar if they plan to stick around. Eventually your regular readers will begin making the requests for you, and you will find that a stronger sense a community develops among those who frequent your site while also contributing to a greater sense of legitimacy in the eyes of new visitors.

As for pictures in general, every post should include at least one visual component relevant to the subject. Ideally, you should post photos of your own, but this should only be done if you have access to a high-resolution camera so that the photos remain clean and crisp. High-quality photos simply make the site appear professional, so if you do not have access to a camera of this quality try to find a relevant photo through a site that provides stock photography.

Graphic Design and Branding

In order to make a strong initial impression on first-time visitors to your blog it is essential to include graphic design elements reflecting your personal brand. A simple but striking image is all that is necessary to accomplish this, but the imagery has to be something relevant to the brand and consistent with the reputation you are trying to establish. This means that the branding should be immediately recognizable and unmistakably associated with you and your blog. This is an opportunity to be creative, but a minimalist approach often remains the best strategy.

Form and Function

Striking the perfect balance between form and function is not the easiest task, so it is to your benefit to constantly evaluate how the design elements you have selected contribute to both the appearance and functionality of the site. Anything that detracts from the site's functionality should be closely examined to ensure that the aesthetic value greatly exceeds the detrimental effect on functionality, and it should indeed be quite rare that aesthetics win out over functionality.

Visitors to the site want to be able to quickly navigate the site to find the specific information they are seeking, so a pleasing but somewhat obtrusive visual will only serve as a deterrent on the whole. Ultimately, your goal should be to create a site that is unmistakably your own but is easily traversed by first-time visitors. Anything that could have an adverse effect on your revenue potential should be eliminated, even if it is something you are quite fond of.

Navigating the Installation Process

High-impact blogging requires a clear dedication to creating a comprehensive and interactive website providing valuable products and services to its audience. Up until this chapter, we have mostly focused on the more technical aspects of blogging without addressing the more detailed components of the process or getting into the actual writing and production work that remains absolutely critical to your success as a blogger.

It is best to have a strong foundation in place and to understand how your blog will be laid out before creating or finalizing the information you intend to make available through your site, as this will enable you to include specific details that make reference to the site design, layout and functionality. With a knowledge of all of the features and capabilities your site possesses, the posts, products and services can all be tailored in a manner that takes full advantage of your blog's resources.

In this chapter we will cover the steps you will take to put the detailed plan you have created into action while going over how to write engaging blog posts that ultimately drive conversions. We will also go over how to create truly valuable digital products and services along with all the different ways those products and services can be leveraged to generate life-changing income. At this point, you will begin to see the value in creating a detailed plan before launching a blog, as your planning and efforts in advance of the launch will ensure a smooth debut and will require relatively few changes or updates once it is established.

Specific Writing Considerations

The most important consideration with regard to the writing

style you choose to employ is your intended target audience. The composition of your target audience will be the deciding factor for the following issues related to your writing style:

- Tone
- Voice
- Level of formality
- Use of technical terminology

Consider the goals you have previously outlined for your site. If you wish to reach the broadest possible audience, then you ought to opt for a simple writing style that is easily understood by all. You may be tempted to impress your readers by demonstrating your mastery of the English language, but the majority of readers will leave the site before they ever bother to open up a dictionary. On the other hand, if you are trying to reach a narrow target audience composed of experts in a particular field, using technical terms and industry-specific jargon will help establish your own level of expertise regarding the subject.

There are methods for achieving a balance as well, particularly if you are trying to educate your audience. When using technical terms relevant to the topic, include a glossary tab in the header and link to the glossary each time you use one of those terms. This will keep readers from leaving the site when they encounter an unfamiliar term and will demonstrate that you care about providing information and guidance to beginners and veterans alike. Always do everything within your power to make the information your blog contains appealing to the widest possible audience if it is possible to do so without sacrificing quality.

Creating Valuable Digital Products

When it comes to potential return on investment, there are few things as valuable as the digital products you create. The only cost associated with producing digital products is the time you invest in its creation, and, if done properly, the return on that initial investment of time can be infinite. In order to yield a substantial return, however, you cannot cut corners or rush to finish the products or services you create. Instead, you have to devote a great deal of time to writing, editing and adding production value before you ever offer it to your readers, whether you intend to offer it for free or for sale.

Your primary focus should be on creating a product that clearly possesses excess value to the reader. This means that the reader will feel as though they got an incredible bargain after buying your digital product or service, which will then lead them to associate your products or services with exceptional value. This is based on the same principle that led publishers (before the advent of widespread digital publishing) to push writers to reach a minimum of 80,000 words before releasing a novel: A buyer is likely willing to pay more for a book that feels weightier than others, and even though the novel could be absolutely perfect at 50,000 words, a reader will simply perceive more value in the work that eclipses the 80,000-word mark.

This does not mean you should cram your work with as many words as possible with no regard to relevance, but it does mean that you should include detailed information and valuable insight a reader may not be likely to find elsewhere. Your selected price point will also play a role in establishing perceived value, but pricing strategies are best discussed as part of developing a promotional strategy for your site, your products and your services.

Developing a Promotional Strategy

Offering free products to readers has long been one of my favorite promotional strategies, but that was not always the case. Early in my career I was asked to offer my assistance on a project that was not supposed to require more than a few hours worth of work. Without going into great detail, I wound up spending several weeks on the project and put a great deal of effort into making sure the client's demands were exceeded in every way possible.

When I was compensated based on the original expectation of just a few hours worth of work, I expressed my disappointment to a more experienced colleague. She laughed, telling me that I should be grateful for the compensation. After all, most people have to pay quite a bit for the right to advertise their skills and expertise. Looking at it from this perspective, I now realize just how valuable free product offerings can be for bloggers. Think of it as a free advertisement that gives readers a clear understanding of what they will get when they pay for your products or services -- and you get the added benefit of a new subscriber to your mailing list.

Focusing on the Finishing Work

It is a common mistake among bloggers to ignore one of the most critical steps involved in the writing process, and even those that understand the importance of editing still fail to do so in a thorough manner. Choosing to neglect the adoption of a detail-oriented approach to editing is tantamount to neglecting to have a home inspected following construction, and the final outcome is just as likely to be disastrous in either circumstance. Not only do minor errors in the writing appear unprofessional, but they can also result in the radical alteration of a sentence's intended meaning.

The last thing you want is to develop a reputation for carelessness, and failing to thoroughly edit and evaluate your work will surely result in this highly undesirable outcome. To most bloggers, the editing and evaluating process is tedious and time-consuming, but the best bloggers -- and the best writers in general -- understand that there is tremendous value in ensuring error-free work that is fine-tuned to a significant degree. In this chapter, we will go over the finishing work necessary for creating a high-impact blog, including the specific editing and evaluative strategies for making sure your work is as strong and as powerful as it should be.

On the Importance of Editing

Poor editing is not always the result of a lack of effort or of a general unwillingness to engage in the process. Self-editing is a notoriously difficult task due to the simple fact that we are keenly aware of what it is we are trying to say through our writing, making it difficult to recognize simple typos, awkward phrasing and a host of other issues that affect the overall quality of the work. This is especially the case if you try to edit your work immediately after you have finished a draft, and, in my view at least, it is best to let your work sit for quite some time before you even attempt to edit or make any changes.

My strategy for editing requires giving your writing some distance, and the amount of distance required will vary among writers. There are times when reading a piece of longform journalism will provide sufficient distance for editing purposes, but there are other times in which it is more ideal to leave your writing alone for several days before you return to edit. Your own writing will seem less familiar the more time passes, allowing you to be more critical and to recognize anything lacking clarity or in need of sweeping changes.

This may seem like a longer process than perhaps is convenient, and it is certainly tempting to just burn through the work until it is complete, allowing you to just kick back and watch your life-changing income roll in. You must recognize, however, that any work you publish is essentially permanent and cannot be changed, so allowing your reputation to be damaged by carelessness will be something you will come to seriously regret. Taking your time to produce quality work by engaging in a patient editing process is the most ideal course of action in the long run.

Evaluating the Inherent Value of the Work

Compared to evaluating the value of your work, editing your work for clarity is unbelievably simple. Most writers will regard their completed work in one of two ways: It is either the absolutely best piece of writing to ever grace the page, or it is the absolutely worst piece of garbage and is unfit for a compost pile, let alone fit for publication. Of course, neither one of these extreme views is usually accurate, which is why it is difficult for writers to honestly evaluate what they have written. So, without an editor or a publisher to offer an honest opinion, how do you evaluate the work you have produced?

For the purpose of high-impact blogging, I have found that it is more than helpful to ask the following evaluative questions regarding the posts and digital products that have been created:

- Is the content volume sufficient? If so, could the information be presented in a more concise manner?
- Does the content include original information or novel concepts unlikely to be found elsewhere?
- Why should consumers be willing to pay for the information included in the content?
- Is the content evergreen or is there a time in the near future when the information will cease to retain its value?

The answers to these questions should help you to recognize when you need to make any changes to the content you have created and whether or not the content is in keeping with the principles of high-impact blogging. If you are still unsure of the accuracy of your personal evaluation, you can always ask friends and family for assistance, or you can opt to enlist the help of an experienced professional for more objective analysis.

Determining When Professional Assistance Is Appropriate

There are several facets of blogging we have discussed that may require professional assistance, but it is often in your best interest to learn how to accomplish these tasks on your own, particularly if you plan to start additional high-impact blogs in the future. If time is a concern or if you feel that your efforts will not yield a worthwhile result, then it may indeed be best to work with a professional. Services that bloggers often outsource typically relate to web design, graphic design, promotional strategy and search-engine optimization. These are skills worth learning, but there are certainly cases in which a pro will be able to generate far greater results for a relatively low cost.

Promoting the Work Without Alienating the Audience

Even if you choose to opt for professional assistance for your promotional strategy, you will still have to engage in some strategies of your own. The best promotional tool at your disposal is adopting a highly personal approach that includes regularly engaging your readers on social media and on your site. You do not have to create additional blog posts or add new products and services on a regular basis, but you do have to be available to answer questions and interact with readers with relative frequency.

By maintaining a presence in the comments section and on social media, you will demonstrate that you truly care about your readers and are willing to put forth extra effort to see them succeed. Many bloggers make the mistake of building a large following on their site and their social media platforms only to alienate their readers by constantly promoting their work without otherwise engaging their readers. To attract and maintain a following, you have to show that you are serious about establishing a long-term, mutually beneficial relationship.

Going Over the Punch List

Finalizing the details relating to your blog is another vital step requiring a great deal of thorough examination and thoughtful reflection. Similar to the process of self-editing and evaluation, going over your punch list can be quite difficult to accomplish with the kind of objectivity necessary to ensure your blog makes the kind of impact that leads to significant and long-term financial success. While it may be helpful to request an objective review from someone who is not directly involved in the project, it is entirely possible to identify and correct any areas of weakness on your own.

In order to accomplish this, it is necessary to be critical and to consider how every aspect of your blog contributes to each intended outcome. Anything that does not clearly and positively contribute to your blog should be summarily dismissed, and the aspects that remain ought to be optimized in a manner that contributes to the achievement of the greatest possible degree of success. This is a trying and time-consuming process that can often be quite frustrating, but it is absolutely essential when it comes to ensuring that you are launching a blog that is effectively positioned for success in both the short and long term.

Ensuring Optimization

It should be quite clear that it is most ideal to set up a blog that requires very little future effort. After all, it is for this specific reason that you have invested so much time in the initial creation of blog posts, products and services, as this makes it possible for you to generate life-changing income while still having the kind of time required to actually enjoy such an exceptional level of income.

In order to ensure that your blog is optimized in a manner oriented to the achievement of this goal, it is necessary for you to review the content you have created and to evaluate whether or not that content has an expiration date. If your posts, products and services lack a sense of timelessness, you should consider modifications to make them evergreen and less reliant on topical information.

Your future time commitment to the site will also be influenced by the monetization strategies you employ, so it is necessary to evaluate whether or not those strategies will generate passive income or if they will require active engagement on your part. Ideally, the products, services and commission-based referrals you provide through your site will require no additional effort once they have been established, as the goal for a high-impact blog is to generate income without commoditizing too much of your time.

Establishing Multiple Paths to Monetization

The primary benefit of implementing a passive income strategy is to create sizable revenue without requiring significant future demands on time, and this is best accomplished through the use of multiple revenue streams. You should be able to offer a variety of digital products and services available through automated site functions, and, if done correctly, digital products and services based on evergreen content will retain their value for the foreseeable future. The result is unlimited income potential based on work that has already been completed, which is the very nature of passive income.

In addition to digital products and services, you may want to consider additional passive income strategies. Many bloggers find a great deal of success through the use of affiliate marketing programs, which can be quite effective when used properly. The key is to adopt a transparent approach and to always maintain a high level of personal integrity when employing this particular strategy, as leading a reader astray just for the sake of a commission will quickly destroy your reputation and adversely affect your ability to earn income through your blog.

You must always be careful when it comes to leveraging the value of your loyal audience, as a lack of transparency may cause your audience to feel as though they are being used or are otherwise being taken advantage of. Nothing can be more alienating to an audience, so use discretion with regard to affiliate marketing and social media promotion.

Revisiting Originality, Value and Future Goals

We have already mentioned the importance of creating original content, but it is a concept vital enough to warrant revisiting it here. Before you even consider launching your site and the products and services it will contain, review the information you plan to dispense and ensure that it possesses clear value to consumers.

For digital content to be valuable, it must contain information that is novel and hard to find elsewhere, and your insights regarding that information must be accurate, interesting and useful. Remember, you have to offer something that is so valuable that those who purchase the product or service are willing to extol its virtues to others. Ideally, these individuals will find your products and services so valuable that they return to your site to look for more, which brings us to the next consideration: Do your offerings encourage future product sales?

High-impact blogging depends on attracting new readers while also retaining existing ones. In order to do this, you have to provide products and services that build upon or expand on prior offerings. This means that you should try to create a series of products that advance from one concept to the next or move from general to specific, as this encourages those satisfied with the initial offering to come back for additional information and insight.

If you are confident in the quality of your work and believe that readers will be thirsting for additional information in short order, then you can make the initial offering available for free. Once your readers recognize that you are providing something valuable, they will happily pay for any additional offerings you make available. This is dependent on your initial planning strategy, as you have to make sure that your content in organized in such a way that it can be delivered in progressive stages that allow the initial concepts to lay the foundation for future ones.

Establishing a Presence in the Marketplace

Once you have all of your content in order and you have launched your site, you have to make sure to establish a firm presence in the marketplace and in the so-called "blogosphere." In the beginning you will have to invest a decent amount of time in this regard, but as you become established and more readily recognizable by your audience and by your peers, you will be able to reap the rewards of the effort you have invested up front without having to commit much additional time at all. This is essentially a "maintenance stage" in which your only real responsibility is to interact with your audience on your site and through social media.

To reach the maintenance stage, you must first establish strong brand recognition among your target audience and among your peers in the industry. This is accomplished through continued promotional strategies specifically designed for this explicit purpose. Many of these promotional strategies require some level of cooperation with other established bloggers, and you may be surprised that the majority of the blogging community is more than willing to assist an aspiring blogger even when that blogger may turn out to be a competitor. This is mostly due to the fact that high-quality blogs add further legitimacy to the perceived expertise of bloggers, which benefits the community as a whole.

Continuing Promotional Strategies

One of the most effective promotional strategies available to a blogger who has just debuted a new site is the guest post. This strategy essentially leverages the audience of another blogger who is already established in the marketplace, and your goal is to present something that benefits all of the involved parties. This means that the guest post you create should be relevant to the site it is posted on and should offer something of value to the community and to the blogger hosting the guest post.

After you have reached out to an established blogger and have landed a guest post spot, make sure you have a topic that is suited to the audience and includes an enticement to your new site. You can offer a free digital product to readers who subscribe to your mailing list or you can simply invite readers to learn more by visiting your site or following you on social media, but there must be some sort of call to action at the end of your guest post to ensure you begin to effectively build an audience.

Sometimes bloggers request a fee for guest posts, sometimes they are free and sometimes you get paid for guest posting. No matter the circumstance, guest posting is a valuable promotional endeavor for quickly attracting an audience to your blog. Most of us do not like the idea of giving our work away for free, but it is important to remember that posts of this kind are among the most effective advertisements for demonstrating your skill and expertise.

Establishing Expert Status

Guest posting is a great way to position yourself as an expert in your field, but the appropriate use of social media is likely the best way to achieve this status in the eyes of the largest possible audience. The fact that interactions and discussions on social media are so easily shared makes it quite easy for you to demonstrate your knowledge and expertise while simultaneously promoting your blog. Of course, social media presents plenty of opportunities to harm your reputation, so it is quite necessary to clearly define what is meant by "appropriate use" of social media.

Any social media account linked to you and your blog should be focused entirely on your brand and your brand alone. If you wish to maintain a personal social media account in order to share the common Internet inanities among friends and family, that is completely acceptable as long as it is separate and not linked in any way to your professional blogging endeavors. This means that you should set the account to private or make use of a pseudonym, as it is of the utmost importance that you maintain a consistently professional reputation throughout your use of social media.

Once you have established separate accounts, always make sure to treat everyone with whom you interact with a great deal of respect. Do not respond to insults or otherwise engage in irrelevant discussions, as this will only serve to harm your reputation. Only engage those posing earnest questions and feel free to chime in on conversations if you have something valuable to add.

In order to take full advantage of social media, make sure your profile contains a link to your site along with a detailed bio explaining your specific area of expertise. By responding with thoughtful and insightful answers provided through social media, you will enhance your reputation as an expert and establish a sense of loyalty among your followers.

Aligning With Other Experts in Your Field

Through guest posting and social media use, you will likely get to know other bloggers in your field. It is best not to regard these bloggers as competitors, as there is very little benefit to an adversarial approach among bloggers. Most people in the blogging community understand that the support of peers results in greater opportunity for all, so try to align with the experts you hold in high regard. This is especially the case if your area of expertise happens to be a subset of a larger category covered by other bloggers.

A blogger who covers criminal law, for example, will take no issue whatsoever with referring their readers to a blogger whose focus is maritime law. The same can be said of an animal care expert referring readers to a blogger covering the care requirements of a specific subset of tropical birds, so try to enlist the assistance of experts in your field with a particular focus on aligning with those covering your topic in a far more generalized manner than you. This will give you their tacit endorsement and a built-in system for referrals, which is quite helpful for establishing a loyal audience for a new blog.

Maintenance, Additions and Value Enhancement

As we have noted previously, the idea behind high-impact blogging is to generate income without having to commoditize a great deal of your future time. On the day your site is launched, the overwhelming majority of the work required will have already been completed, but there are still aspects requiring continued maintenance and updates. There is also the question of whether or not you will want to continue to create added value by leveraging your initial success to include other platforms.

Most of the general blog maintenance and the associated technical issues should be easily addressed through automated systems or with very little effort on your part. Your main responsibility after your site has debuted and you have attracted a sizable audience is to continue to engage your audience on both the blog and on social media. This does not require your constant presence, but taking the time to respond to messages and to interact with your audience on a daily basis can be highly beneficial in terms of your blog's overall success.

Keeping Monetization Strategies Updated and Efficient

Using passive income strategies is attractive because of the minimal effort required on the part of the blogger. Even though this is the case, there are still instances in which updates can be highly beneficial and are certainly encouraged. However, if you have your posts and products already in place and generating income, why should you have to keep updating your site with new information when you are content with the revenue that is coming in?

The main reason to do so is to retain your audience over a longer period of time and to offer new insight on topics you have already addressed. One way to do this is by revisiting one of your original posts and adding something new or offering a note of clarification, thereby causing visitors who have already read the post to re-read it for the updated information. If those readers did not respond to the initial call to action but were intrigued by it and considered responding, an update to the post may spur them to take action, thereby generating revenue that would have been missed out on otherwise.

There is also the added benefit of repeat visitors seeing that the site is not static, ensuring that any new product offerings or other additions will be seen by the whole of your audience. This, along with your continued activity in the comments section of your blog posts and also on social media, will help you retain audience members who find your content valuable and wish to benefit from any future updates or additions you integrate into the site.

Using Other Platforms for Added Reach

Expanding your work to include other platforms is an option you may wish to consider if you want to reach a larger audience and are comfortable investing additional time to do so. In much the same way as the setup for a high-impact blog can be accomplished by doing the majority of the work up front in order to generate passive income after the launch, many of the other platform options can be set up similarly. The goal, of course, should be to utilize these platforms without spreading yourself thin, so carefully consider the timing of adding these new platforms to complement the work you do through your blog.

There are many platforms at your disposal, and the most ideal choice to add will depend on the audience you wish to target. Of them all, the safest best is likely podcasting, and the platform itself is ideal regardless of whether you wish to adopt a passive income strategy or plan to take a more active approach that allows you to include topical information relevant to your chosen subject. Whatever platform you ultimately choose to utilize, make sure to invest in quality materials in order to maintain your reputation for professionalism.

Strategies for Growth and Value Enhancement

It is possible to further leverage your success as a blogger into additional opportunities for generating revenue. In order to enhance your personal value and the value of your blog, some of these strategies do require the commoditization of your future time. As such, you will have to make a decision whether you wish to invest your time in this way, but these opportunities are almost entirely worthwhile, particularly due to their lucrative nature.

One particular strategy for continued growth and value enhancement is creating and offering new digital products through the site. This may be a necessary component of maintenance, but it is also an excellent way to ensure the continued growth of your site. Of course, true value enhancement requires a bit of diversification, which is why it is important to seriously consider opting for a strategy that includes products and services that are presented in a manner different from previous product and service offerings.

Speaking engagements and e-courses are excellent options in this regard, especially when you have already established a sizable following. At first glance, an in-person speaking engagement seems like an inefficient monetization strategy due to capacity limits dictating a strict ceiling on revenue generation, but this built-in limit can be bypassed by simply recording the session and creating a digital product using the live footage. This is also the case with live e-courses, as your earning potential is not limited by the number of people who sign up since you can simply record and reuse the footage for future sale on the site.

In order to properly leverage these strategies, it is important to promote the benefit of your direct instruction and guidance in real time. This will be particularly appealing for your most loyal followers, as they will be keenly interested in direct interaction with the person responsible for creating the digital products and services that have benefitted them so much already. These sessions can also be used as promotional tools for attracting new readers, especially when you create a comprehensive course taught by multiple experts in your field.

www.ingramcontent.com/pod-product-compliance
Lightning Source LLC
Chambersburg PA
CBHW020949180526
45163CB00006B/2375